Condomania

101 uses for a Condom

by Peter Maddocks

From a disgusting idea by Simon Maddocks

Robson Books

First published in Great Britain in paperback in 1987 by Robson
Books Ltd, Bolsover House, 5-6 Clipstone Street, London W1P 7EB.

Second impression May 1987   Ninth impression June 1989
Third impression May 1987   Tenth impression April 1990
Fourth impression May 1987   Eleventh impression July 1990
Fifth impression August 1987   Twelfth impression May 1991
Sixth impression October 1987   Thirteenth impression November 1991
Seventh impression December 1987   Fourteenth impression October 1992
Eighth impression January 1988

British Library Cataloguing in Publication Data

Maddocks, P.
   Condomania: 101 uses for a condom.
   1. English wit and humour, Pictorial
   I. Title
   741.5'942   NC1479

   ISBN 0-86051-451-X

Printed in Great Britain by St Edmundsbury Press Ltd, Bury St
Edmunds, Suffolk.

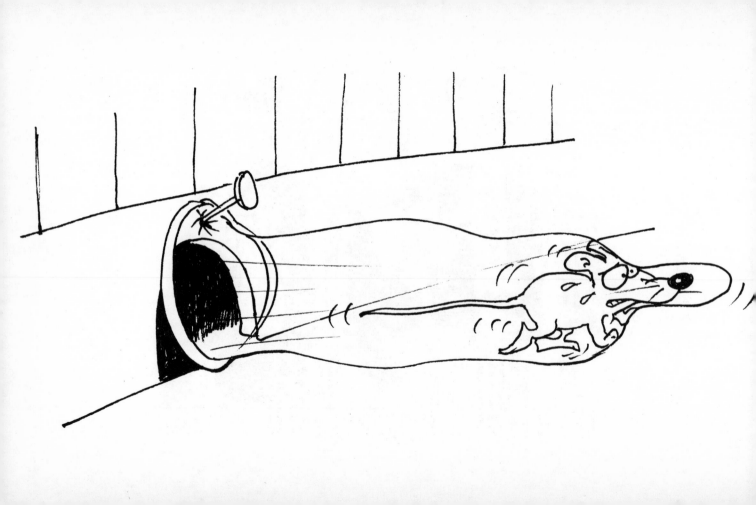

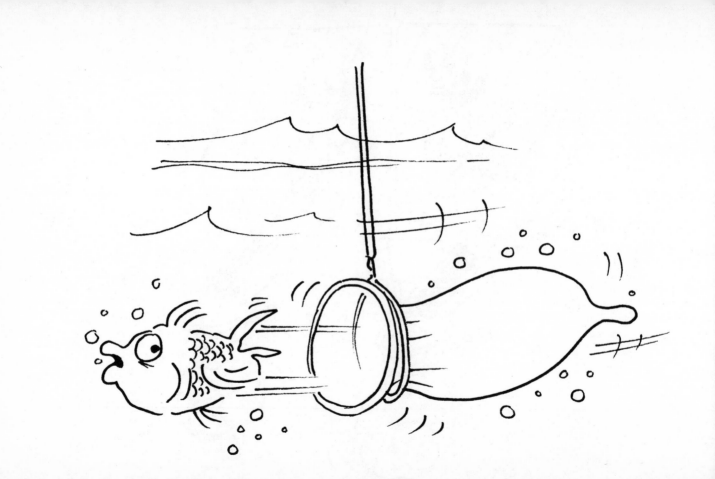

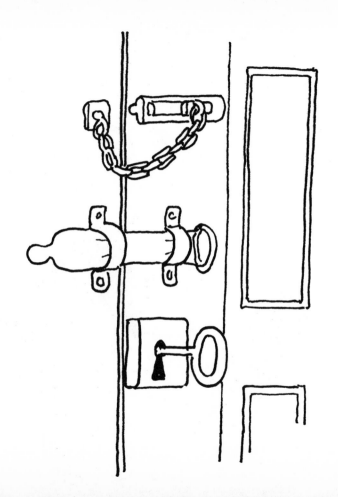

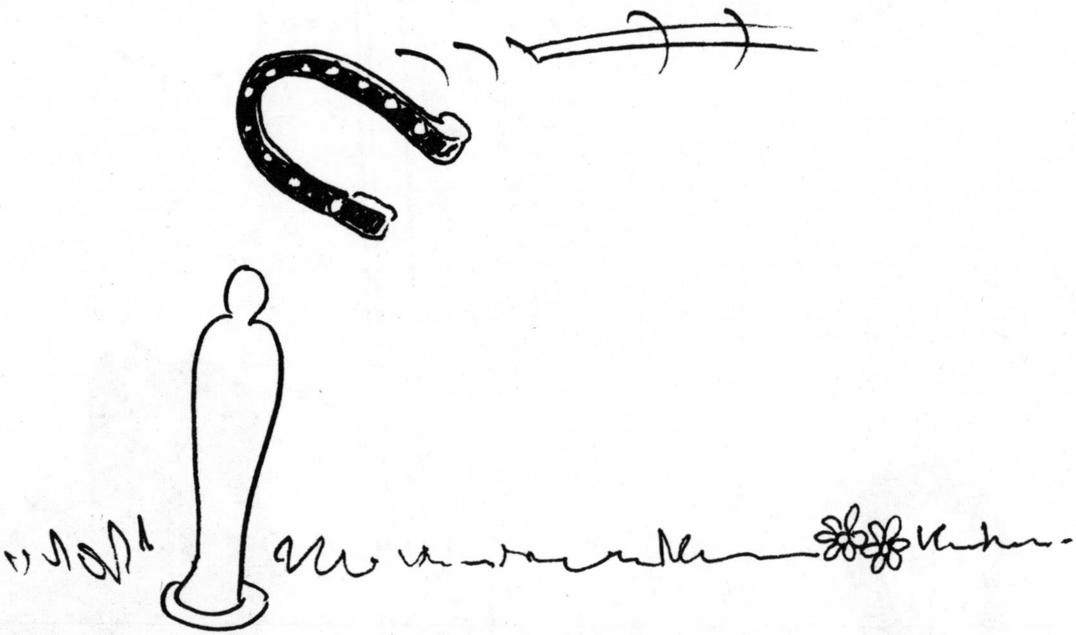

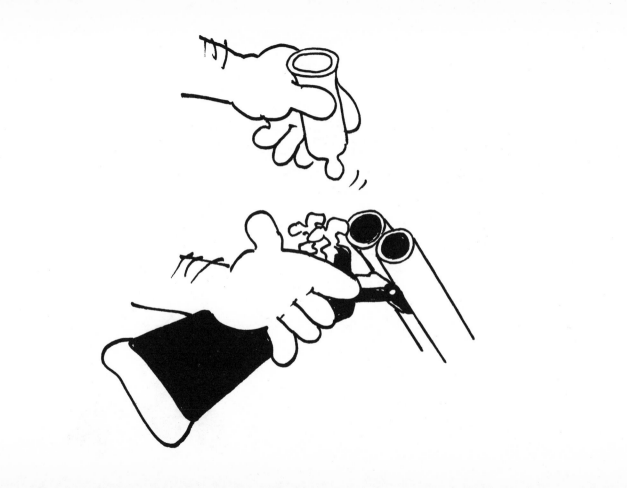

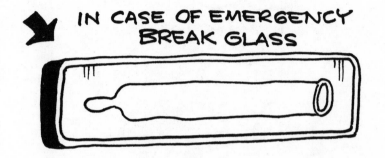

IN CASE OF EMERGENCY
BREAK GLASS

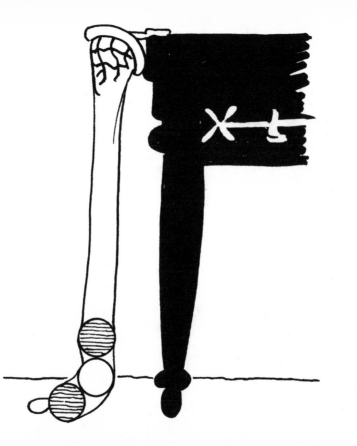

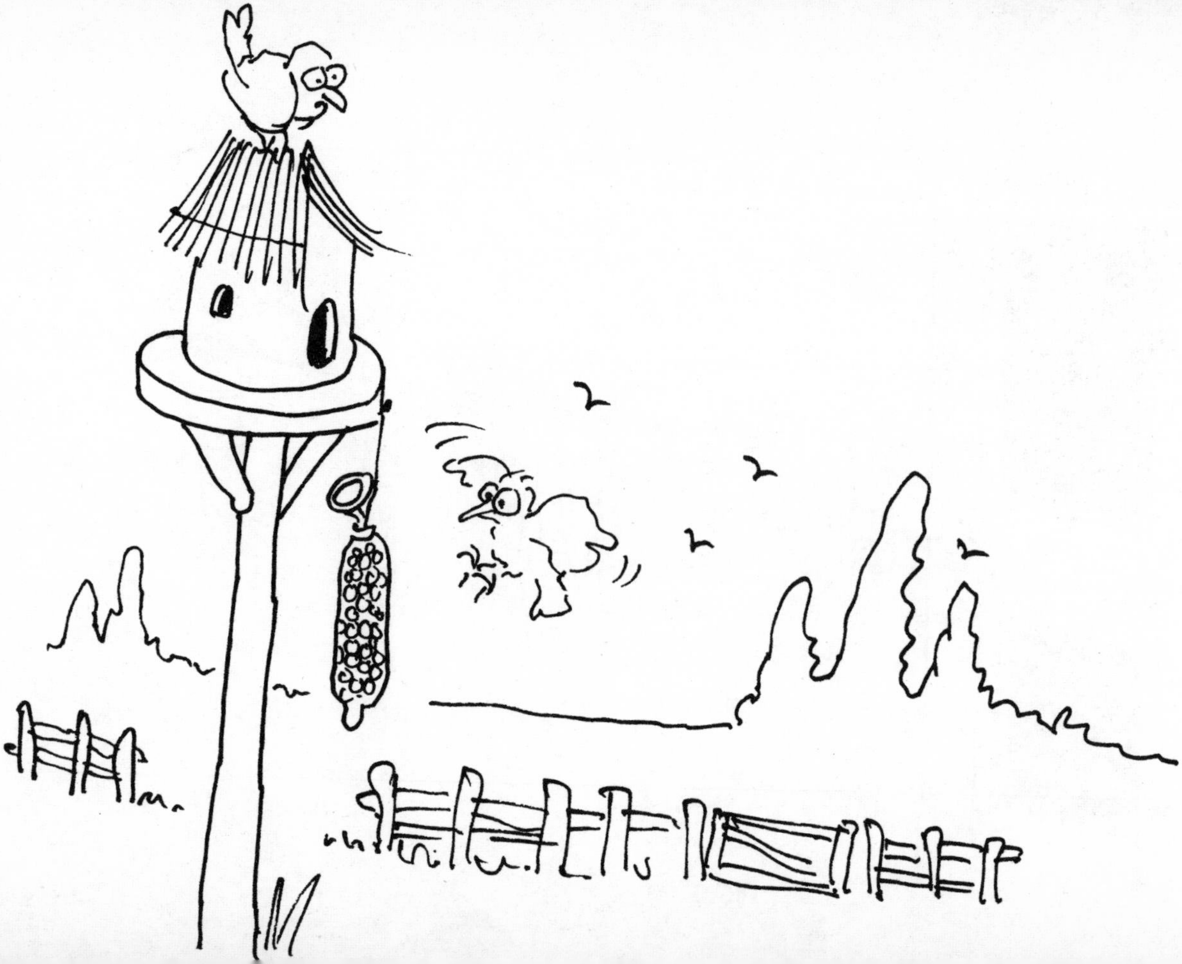

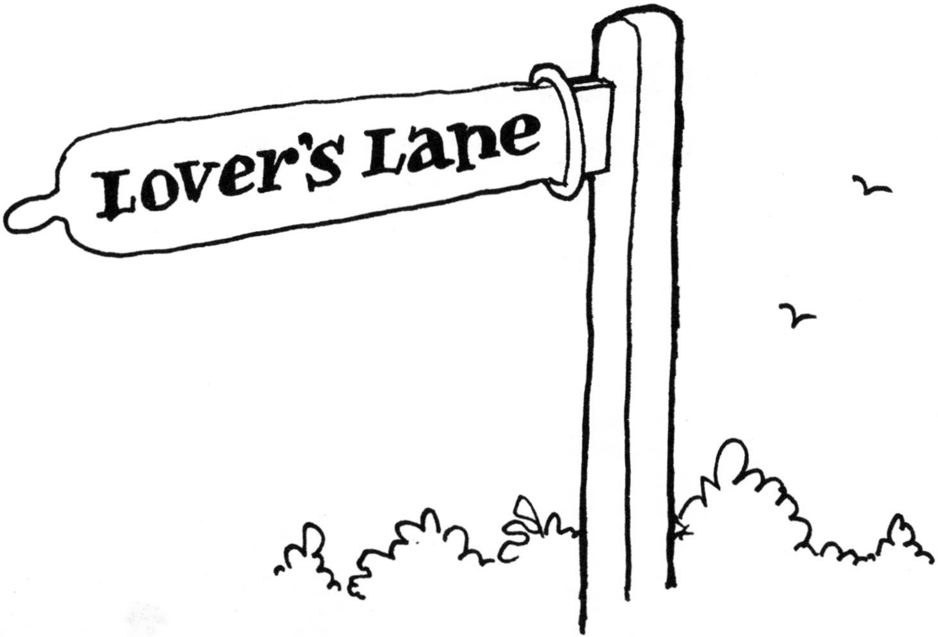
Lover's Lane

PS...

there is another use for
the Condom — but I'm
going to leave that to
your own vivid Imagination...

CONTRIBUTIONS FROM:
Simon Maddocks
Keith Learner